Y0-BBC-357

WORLD OF RACING

CHAMP CARS

By Sylvia Wilkinson

Consultants:
John Morton
Wiley McCoy
Jonesy Morris
Roman Kuzma

CHILDRENS PRESS, CHICAGO

Danny Sullivan

Picture Acknowledgments

Jan Bigelow—2, 4 (4 photos), 8, 9 (top), 11 (bottom), 20, 25 (right), 26, 32 (2 photos), 35 (left), 37, 43

Indianapolis Motor Speedway Corporation—7, 9, 11 (top), 13 (2 photos, middle and bottom), 31

Ernie Lovingood—13 (top)

Tom Winter—15, 28, 39

Wayne Hartman—17 (3 photos)

Yoshi Suzuka—19, 23

Dennis Torres—19, 25 (left)

Candee & Associates—35 (right)

Sylvia Wilkinson—40

Dave Hutson—Cover (4 photos)

Library of Congress Cataloging in Publication Data
Wilkinson. Sylvia, 1940-
   Champ cars.
  (World of racing)
   Summary: Covers driving in the annual Indianapolis 500, developments in racing cars, and the work of pit crews.
    1. Automobile racing—Juvenile literature.
2. Indianapolis Speedway Race—Juvenile literature. 3. Automobiles, Racing—Juvenile literature. [1. Indianapolis Speedway Race.
2. Automobile racing. 3. Automobiles, Racing]
I. Title. II. Series.
GV1029.W494   796.7'2   81-7687
ISBN 0-516-04711-6   AACR2

Copyright© 1982 by Regensteiner Publishing Enterprises, Inc.
All rights reserved. Published simultaneously in Canada.
Printed in the United States of America.

1 2 3 4 5 6 7 8 9 10 R 91 90 89 88 87 86 85 84 83 82

THE INDY 500

What is the most famous one day sporting event in the world? There is only one answer—the Indianapolis 500.

Except during the two World Wars, the race has been held in Indianapolis, Indiana since 1911. On Memorial Day each spring, the Indy 500 attracts drivers from all over the world. They compete for the richest purse in racing; more than $300,000 goes to the winner. Although past winners have come from many countries, Indy is an American event and an American kind of racing.

The ninety-two garages that make up the famous "Gasoline Alley" teem with activity the month of May as mechanics prepare their cars for practice and qualifying. Tiny, ten-horsepower tractors chug around the pits like tugboats, pulling the powerful Champ cars whose engines when fired up for a track run put out over 700 horsepower.

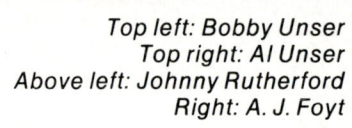

Top left: Bobby Unser
Top right: Al Unser
Above left: Johnny Rutherford
Right: A. J. Foyt

The sun goes in and out. The rain falls frequently on the Indiana cornfields and on the asphalt track, making the farmers happy and the racers anxious. Nerves tighten during the wait for a qualifying attempt: ten miles, four laps around the two-and-a-half mile track.

Famous names are at the Speedway with their teams and cars, such as multiple winners of the big purse: Johnny Rutherford, A. J. Foyt, and the Unser brothers, Al and Bobby. Rookie tests take place for the newcomers under the watchful eyes of the officials and veteran drivers. Rookies and veterans alike who haven't landed a ride for the race mill around the pits and garages, hoping to be tapped for a tryout. Destined to become one of the great Indy drivers, Eddie Sachs once took a job washing dishes in the Speedway restaurant, just to be near the action.

We are going to Indy in the driver's seat with National Champion Tom Sneva and former Super Vee champion Dennis Firestone, a newcomer in Champ cars. They drive the powerful, single seat cars which with engines no larger than a small economy car are race-prepared to reach speeds of over 200 miles per hour. We will find out about car construction, driving techniques, safety, and pit stops.

So, "Ladies and Gentlemen, start your engines!"

A NEW DRIVER AT INDY

"Indianapolis, from the first time I saw it," Dennis Firestone remembers, "was awesome."

Dennis, who is one of the most successful Super Vee drivers in America, won twenty-three National races in a row. One day after racing the Mini-Indy race for Super Vees at nearby Indianapolis Raceway Park, Dennis went over to the Indianapolis Speedway to take a look. The Champ cars were qualifying for the yearly event.

"I stood by the track, watching the cars go by at incredible speeds, listening to the sounds, and I got chills all over. Right then I said, 'I've got to do this.'"

When Dennis got the chance to drive a Champ car at Indy, he fulfilled the dream of many American boys and girls. It was a day he'll never forget.

Official photograph of Dennis Firestone at the Indianapolis 500

"You're there for a whole month before Memorial Day, testing, qualifying, getting ready. I remember the first day I arrived at the track, the twenty-eighth of April. The first thing I saw was the Hall of Fame. The track was empty. No one was in the grandstands. I had seen this place on TV since I was a kid. I couldn't believe I was really here. I was saying, 'I've got a car. I'm going to race at Indianapolis.' What a feeling that was!

"Then, after all the work and waiting for race day, all the buildup on your nerves, on race morning I felt strangely cut off from it. I was in the garage with my car. I didn't see the pageantry going on outside, the marching bands, the prerace celebration, the fans. I wasn't a part of it. I was so nervous, I had this small perspective that didn't include what was going on outside. Just me and this race car.

"I started the car for the parade lap. I was moving around the track and I looked up in front of me. There were six or seven rows of cars that had qualified ahead of me, beautifully colored, shiny cars. As I exited turn four and moved towards the start/finish line, all of a sudden it hit me. There were people everywhere, colored balloons were floating into the sky. Engines were rumbling. And out in front of me was this narrow, black strip of ribbon. This was it. At that moment, it was real. For a short moment before the flag dropped and I started racing, it really got me. This was Indianapolis!"

Dennis Firestone (75) races Geoff Brabham (21)

THE BEGINNING OF INDY

When Carl Fisher first dreamed up the Indy 500, he decided that 500 miles was a good length because the race could be finished in one day. He also decided to have a big purse for the drivers so that Indy would never have to play second fiddle to any other race. His plan was perfect. Today Indy is still the richest, biggest race in the world.

Early champ cars carried a driver and a mechanic.

The first race in 1911 paid $14,000 to the winner, enough to buy a mansion in those days. Today, over a million dollars is paid to the competitors. The first 500 miles was run in six hours and forty-two minutes. Today the racers finish the distance in less than half that time. Nowadays, when the first driver completes 500 miles, the checkered flag is given and the race ends. In the old days, the other drivers could keep going until they too completed 500 miles. Ralph Mulford, who finished tenth in 1912, raced for three hours after all the other drivers had stopped and the spectators had gone home. In this second 500, Ralph De Palma got out and pushed his Mercedes when the engine failed while he was leading. He finally abandoned the car and proudly went the last 600 yards on foot.

Although Indy is American racing, foreign drivers have participated and often won. From 1912 to 1920, not a single American won the crown. In 1913, the French driver, Goux, who won the race by a large margin, continued to drive at full speed even though his American mechanics kept waving the sign "Retardez"—slow down, in French.

Above: Jules Goux, winner of the 1913 Indianapolis 500.
Below: Herm Johnson in an Eagle-Chevrolet

THE CHAMP CAR

The cars that run at Indy are called either Indy, Championship, or Champ cars. They have one seat, no fenders, and are powered by an engine in the rear. The history of Champ cars is marked by three revolutionary changes: *rear engines, monocoque construction,* and *ground effects.* Let's examine the changes that have affected all modern racing cars.

From the twenties to the fifties Americans took a strong hold on Indy. But a change was taking place in Grand Prix racing, the international road racing series, that was soon to change Indy forever. Engines were being moved from in front of the driver to the rear.

The traditional Indy "roadster" was a sturdy vehicle. It weighed a ton, was thirteen feet long and twenty-one inches high. It was made of strong steel tubing with aluminum body panels. It had thirty-two pounds of nuts and bolts holding it together. All of the cars used the same engine, the four cylinder Offy built by Dale Drake and Louis Meyer. The cars were very similar so an outstanding driver could easily be picked out of the pack.

Top: Pre-roadster race cars often used the Offy engine.
Middle: Mauri Rose won the 1947 Indy 500 in this roadster.
Bottom: Jack Brabham's 1961 Cooper-Climax was the first successful rear-engine car to race at Indy.

Rear Engines

When the rear engined car of Jack Brabham of Australia arrived at Indy in 1961, it immediately earned the nickname "Funny Car." In earlier races, engines had been turned on their sides in an attempt to make the cars more aerodynamic but this didn't work well. When the world Champion driver, Brabham, took his funny car around the track, even the strongest doubters knew the day of the old roadsters was coming to a close.

Brabham's car had much less power since its Climax engine was 85 cubic inches smaller than the 252 cubic inch American engines. It had independent suspension on all four wheels. Veteran Indy mechanic Clint Brawner exclaimed: "That car is so low it makes our roadsters resemble Mack trucks."

But Brawner was not a doubter. He knew that the low, aerodynamic car with its phenomenal ability to stick in the turns was the car of the future. He knew the reason Brabham only placed seventh in the race was because his crew was inexperienced at quick tire changes and refueling.

In 1963, the great English designer Colin Chapman, who is still designing winning cars today in Formula One, brought over two Lotus-Ford cars. The Lotus chassis was unique in

Close-up of a rear engine and monocoque in a Champ car.

many ways. The engine was close to the middle of the car between the driver and in front of the gearbox. The driver drove in a reclining position. In the standard front engined roadster, the driver drove in an upright position so he could see over the engine. The driver's line of sight in the Lotus was no more than a foot and a half off the ground, below the top of the tires. Also the Firestone Tire Company had made special "low profile" racing tires for the car. Scottish World champion Jimmy Clark finished second at Indy and first at Milwaukee in this funny car. By 1965, over half the field had decided the funny car was the fastest way to go. Today all of the Champ cars are rear engined.

Monocoque

The Lotus of Chapman brought another development to American racing — the monocoque. The Lotus was not made of heavy steel tubing with aluminum panels bolted on like the roadsters. The center structure was made like the fuselage of an airplane with its strength coming from its "stressed skin" construction. This was the forerunner of today's cars, which weigh about 1,500 pounds, 500 pounds less than the front engined roadsters.

On today's cars, the monocoque center structure is covered with a fiberglass body. Fiberglass is a hard, lightweight material that is formed in molds. Here are the construction stages for a fiberglass body for a modern racing car.

First a wooden buck is built to form the framework for the body.

Next, foam is put between the stations or cross members that divide the buck into sections.

After that, workmen shape the foam from station to station.

Then fiberglass is put over the whole structure. The structure is built 1/4" undersize so there is room to put the fiberglass on. Bondo, a body putty, is used over the fiberglass to smooth the finish. This is called the plug.

Finally a mold is made from the plug so that many body panels can be made.

First a wooden buck (top) is built to form the framework for the body. Next a white foam is put between the stations or cross members (right). Then fiberglass is put over the whole structure. Bondo is used to smooth the finish. This is the plug (below). You can see the finished product on page 25.

Ground Effects

A conventional or flat-bottom car depends on wings on the front and rear for its downforce. Bobby Unser once drove this Eagle, a flat-bottom car with a large rear wing and smaller nose wings.

The first ground effects or curved bottom Champ car was the PC7 introduced by Roger Penske in 1979.

How does a ground effects car work? First we need to understand how a *wing* works. A wing has a curved surface. A race car wing curves more on the bottom than on the top. An airplane wing does the opposite. A race car wing is designed to produce *downforce,* the force that makes a car stick to the ground while speeding through curves. An airplane wing causes *lift,* the force that lifts the plane off the ground when fast moving air passes across its wings. How can a curved surface cause an airplane to lift and a race car to stick to the ground?

Look at the side views of a race car wing and an airplane wing. When fast moving air passes under the race car wing, the curved surface causes the air to become thinner. Although the air across the top and the air across the bottom are going the same speed, the air across the bottom has farther to go. As the air gets thinner, an area of low air pressure is produced. The higher pressure air on the top can push down harder. This makes the car stick better to the ground.

A ground effects race car uses a large curved area under the bottom of the car, making it like a giant wing. The curved bottom area on most Champ cars is under the *sidepods.* Sidepods are the structures between the front and rear wheels.

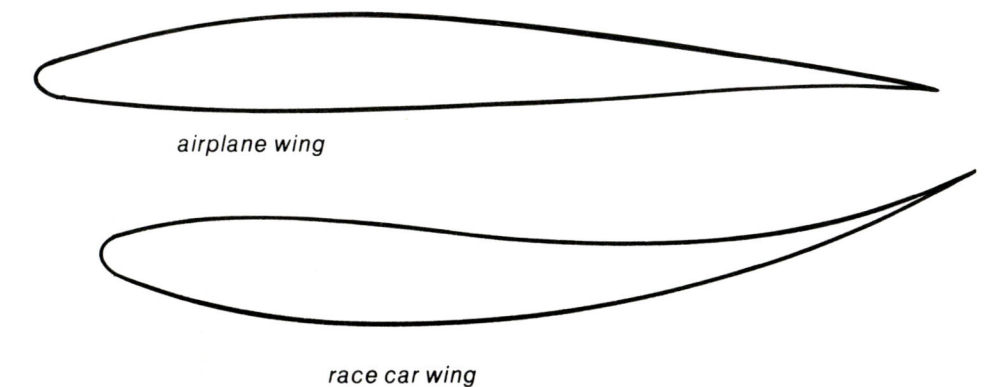

airplane wing

race car wing

Dennis Firestone and Tony Bettenhauser (6)

Dennis explains: "Earlier when I drove a flat-bottom or non-ground effects car, I would put on my brakes for a turn and feel a ground effects car go past me. I would already have to be slowed down to make the turn while the ground effects car would still be sailing into it, the driver knowing that his car would stick and make the turn."

Though the results are different, Tom Sneva says that the feel of driving a ground effects car is the same as a flat-bottom car. "Only the *g-forces* on your body tell you it's any different," he relates. "And the speed increase, which at Indy can be seven to nine miles an hour."

In a race car, the g-forces or gravity forces that Tom feels acting on his body occur when he corners, accelerates, and brakes. Because a ground effects car corners faster and stops better than a conventional car, the driver feels his body strain against these motions.

CHAMP CAR TRACKS

The earliest car races in America took place on two types of courses: the open road and closed circuit tracks. Most of the closed tracks were wooden or dirt. When Carl Fisher staged the first race in Indianapolis, many accidents took place because the track was filled with chuck holes. These holes caused tires to blow out and also tipped over the cars, dumping out the drivers and the riding mechanics.

Although there was bad publicity because several people were killed at this first event, Fisher put more thought into his idea. The dirt track would have to be done away with. Because concrete couldn't stand the hard Indianapolis winter, he decided on brick. This is how Indy became known as the Brickyard. Today only one yard of the original brick is left showing at the start/finish line. The rest is covered with modern asphalt. To mark the opening day, one "brick of gold" was laid (actually bronze and brass) then removed and put into the Speedway Museum.

Today Champ cars are run on two types of tracks: *oval* and *road courses*. Let's look first at ovals.

Actually the most famous oval of them all — Indy — isn't exactly an oval. It is more of a rectangle with rounded corners. The track is two and a half miles long and between each of the four corners is a straight. The long straights are five-eighths of a mile and the short straights are one-eighth. Each of the turns is one-quarter of a mile. Add that up and you'll find that the cars are on straights for a mile and a half and in corners for a mile. As with all ovals, the turns are all left-handers.

A popular variation of the oval shape is the *tri-oval* such as Pocono and Michigan. Champ cars return to the same tracks, with the exception of Indy, many times a year. This is part of the reason that more and more races are being held today on *road courses*.

Road courses such as Riverside are tracks that contain a variety of turns both left and right-handers, with elevation changes and varying widths and lengths. In the past Champ cars were built for turning left only. Today, since all of the new Champ cars have come from Formula One designs and technology, they are more like Grand Prix cars than in the past. Also road racing is becoming more popular in North America. The use of road racing tracks gives the Champ cars more places to race and an audience they have not had before.

INDIANAPOLIS MOTOR SPEEDWAY

- Short straight
- Corner
- Long straight
- Indy is more of a rectangle with corners than an oval. It has two short straights and two long straights between the corners.
- 2.5 miles

POCONO

This is a 2.5 mile tri-oval with a 2.8 road course.

DARLINGTON

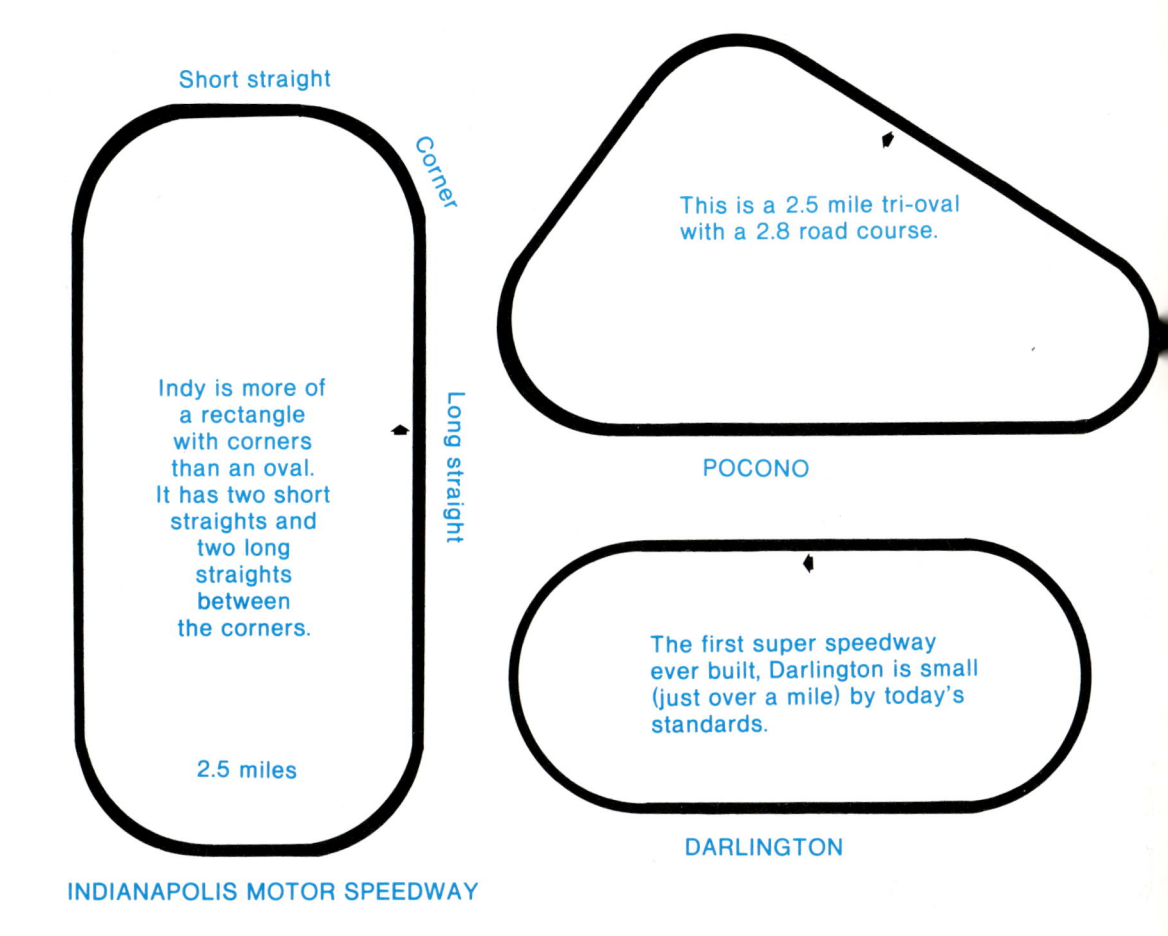

The first super speedway ever built, Darlington is small (just over a mile) by today's standards.

Champ cars have a special problem that prevents them from racing on famous ovals such as Daytona, Talledega, or Darlington. While a stock car would reach a speed of 195 at Daytona, a Champ car would run 220 to 230 miles per hour. But it would not run those speeds safely. Champ cars are too fragile and the road surface too rough. Also the g-loads, the forces that Tom Sneva spoke of in high speed cornering and accelerating, would be dangerously high.

DRIVING A 500 MILE RACE

Two-time winner of the 500 Bill Vukovich, a man who never minced words, once said: "All you have to do to win Indy is keep your foot on the throttle and turn left." Dennis and Tom say it isn't that simple.

Dennis explains: "A race car becomes a part of your body like a finger or a hand. You shouldn't have to think about shifting, braking, or turning. The mechanics of driving a car must become as automatic as picking up a cup of coffee." Yet Dennis remembers his first Champ car race when he felt as though he were starting over. "Super Vee gave me racing experience, but until I drove a Champ car, I couldn't possibly imagine how important the element of horsepower is. I went 160 in a Super Vee, so I thought 190 in a Champ car shouldn't be so different. That's only 30 miles an hour faster, I told myself. Well, that 30 miles an hour faster made the Champ car feel like it was *twice* as fast as the Super Vee.

"My whole driving style had to be readjusted. A Super Vee can be tolerant, forgiving. I could be abrupt in moving up and down and around on the track very freely. Super Vees don't

Janet Guthrie was the first woman to race at the Indy 500.

create turbulence behind them. You move in behind a Champ car and if you follow too closely, the effect on you is violent. You're shaking around in the cockpit. Your vision is blurred. It feels as if the air could rip your helmet off."

Driving a 500 mile race is a special kind of endurance test for both car and driver. In a 500 mile race today, Tom says: "A driver must try hard all the time. With today's cars and competition, a 500 mile race is just a long sprint race. You still have a long distance strategy, but for example if you have a problem early in the race, you have a tendency to think you'll never be able to win. This isn't true. You have to force yourself to keep pressing hard because you can never guess what might happen in the race."

When you watch the Indy 500 on TV, cars go around almost mechanically like toys on a slot car track. You see the inevitable spinouts, blowouts, and accidents that send cars out of control and often into the wall.

Gordon Johncock (20), Mario Andretti (40) in Wildcats and Bill Whittington (94) in a March at Indy. All three use the Cosworth DFX. Johncock won the 1982 Indy 500 by only .16 of a second, the closest finish in the history of the race.

"Mental fatigue in a long race is far more of a problem than physical fatigue," Tom explains. "Your hands, arms, and feet keep working if your brain tells them the right things to do. Your brain is what you have to struggle with, keeping the kind of intense concentration you must have to drive a Champ car. Even the tiniest mistake at those speeds can be a disaster. You see, speed becomes relative. You get used to it. You learn to relax on the straights."

Imagine relaxing at 200 miles an hour!

Dennis agrees with Tom. "It is crucial not to let your concentration fade during a race." You are traveling at a rate of over 300 feet per second in a Champ car. If you lose concentration for only one second, you go more than the length of a football field.

"During the course of a 500 mile race, conditions change completely," Dennis relates. "Spectators might think they are just watching cars go round and round, 200 times the same way, but from the driver's viewpoint, every time you go around, more oil is on the track, more rubber is in a turn. The longer you go, the hotter your car gets. With heat your tire pressures change so the handling of the car changes. Nothing is more tiring than having to continue to drive fast with a car that isn't performing properly."

Tom adds, "You start a race with a strategy or game plan. Then the race gets underway and things start happening. There will be caution flags, maybe car problems or a slow pit stop for you. All of this dictates the course of the race and you must change your strategy as you go."

Tom, a former middle school principal, understands the mental effort of both reading books and driving race cars: "The mental effort in a long race is like reading a novel and being told you have to remember 99 percent of what you read. At Indy your body interferes with the effort of your brain. For instance, if it is 80 degrees at Indianapolis in the stands, it is 110 degrees inside the race cars.

Pit stops can win or lose a race.

"Changing your pace is also difficult. You are driving 200 and you have to make a pit stop. Slowing down to 100 in the pit lane feels almost like stopping, like driving your street car around town. Late in the race, many tired drivers have trouble judging when and where to stop in their pits."

Crew man Jonesy Morris agrees: "It is easy for a driver to accidentally slide through his designated pit. He has become so used to high speeds and not used to coming to a complete stop that he can come into the pit lane too hot. He can sail through with all four wheels locked up."

Clint Brawner, twenty-five-year veteran of Indy who has prepared cars for such famous drivers as Mario Andretti and A. J. Foyt, says: "Indy's 500 miles add up to equivalent of 100,000 normal highway miles." Of the thirty-three cars that start the 500 every year, two thirds will not be running at the finish.

In the past there have been heartbreaking stories of cars and drivers that didn't make the last few miles. In 1961, Eddie Sachs's wife was on her way to meet him in Victory Circle when Sachs led the race with only a few miles to go. Suddenly a strip of rubber rolled off his right rear tire. Rather than risk a blowout and a possible crash, he made a pit stop for a new tire. He lost to A. J. Foyt by eight seconds. A wheel hammer went flying into the air after his stop; some say it was stuck to the new wheel, but some say it was heaved at him by his frustrated mechanic as he exited the pits.

With only seven miles to go in 1967, Parnelli Jones's turbine car broke a fifty cent part in the gearbox and failed to finish. In 1920 when many cars were dropping out because a certain factory had failed to heat-treat parts to strengthen them, one of the Chevrolet brothers, Gaston, won the race. His brother, Louis, exasperated at the failure of their other cars, said, "Well, thank goodness this didn't break, too." He angrily kicked the steering arm on his brother's winning Monroe car. To their surprise, the part broke and clattered to the ground!

Safety

Racing has produced many safety items. In 1937, a process used in the aircraft industry called *Magnaflux* came to racing. Magnaflux is used to locate internal flaws and cracks that might cause a part to fail under stress.

A safety device first used on race cars at Indy was the rear-view mirror, used by the first winner in 1911, Ray Harroun. Most drivers had a riding mechanic in the passenger seat who would warn the driver when a car was approaching from the rear to attempt to pass. Harroun wanted to eliminate the need for this passenger so he devised a mirror over the dashboard of his car that would afford him a rear view. This device that is taken for granted today on all cars seemed very strange in 1911.

All race cars today use a driver restraint or seat belt system. In the past few years, lap and shoulder belts have been added to passenger cars.

Safety fuel containers are also used in Champ cars. Inside the tanks are special bladders that keep fuel from spilling in an accident. Also inside the tank is a foam that prevents sloshing. In order to have a "crash worthy" fuel system, Indy cars use a bladder similar to that used on military helicopters. Even a bullet will not penetrate it.

Gaston Chevrolet, winner of the 1920 race at Indianapolis.

Early racers at Indy used wire wheels or wheels with spokes instead of a solid metal wheel. But spoked wheels are not strong, so many of the wheels broke. In 1941, former Indy winner Wilbur Shaw found a badly out of balance wheel in his garage. He marked the wire wheel with chalk and told his crew not to use it. On race day, a terrible garage fire started when gasoline used to wash parts was ignited by a spark from a welder. The fire hoses washed away Shaw's chalk mark. During the race, the spokes in a wheel broke and Shaw crashed, breaking his back. He always thought that the broken wheel must have been the one he had marked with chalk.

31

In 1952, after the famous Italian driver Alberto Ascari broke a wire wheel on his Ferrari and spun into the infield, wire wheels were banned for competition. As technology advanced in wheel construction and design, light alloy castings were developed that were light as well as strong.

Wilbur Shaw, who was the first man to drive 200 mph on the straight at Indy, was laughed at by his fellow drivers for wearing a metal helmet instead of the traditional aviation cloth or leather cap. But even Shaw wouldn't wear a seat harness, preferring to duck when the car overturned. Today's drivers wear very advanced safety gear from helmets that give them air when there is fire to suits that can resist flames for thirty seconds.

Gordon Johncock (left) and Vern Schuppan (below) wear protective clothing and helmets.

Rookie Tests

Rookie tests for new drivers became a rule in the mid-thirties. Results had shown that new drivers at Indy had been involved in all but four of the serious accidents from 1930 to 1935 that took the lives of nine drivers and six mechanics.

Dennis recalls his rookie test: "At first I didn't think it was a good idea, but now I'm glad I had to do it.

"The test falls into two parts. For the first test, you must run twenty consecutive laps at 160 miles an hour. You can refuel during that time, but you cannot let your speed vary more than three miles an hour.

"For the second test, your speed goes up. But it is not important to go extremely fast. You must run 170 or over and, again, not vary your speed more than three miles an hour. They aren't interested in seeing if you can run 180; just that you can turn nice, consistent laps. After you're done, you go into a critique session with the chief steward and the four veteran drivers who watched you on each turn. The test teaches you discipline most of all. It stops a rookie from going too fast, too soon. You work your speed up gradually, seeing what is going on around you a little at a time. You get the feel of it without scaring yourself with too much speed."

Alcohol

Many types of fuel have been used at Indy: gasoline, kerosene, and methanol (alcohol). In 1914, Willie Carlson, driving a Maxwell, ran the cheapest 500 miles in history when he used thirty gallons of kerosene at six cents a gallon. In the early days at Indy most cars used gasoline, so the garage area became known as "Gasoline Alley."

In 1940, three-time Indy winner Wilbur Shaw used methanol instead of gasoline. Methanol is a synthetic alcohol. He found it kept the engine temperature down. Methanol is still used today. Engine builder Wiley McCoy tells why: "When alcohol mixes with air and vaporizes for the combustion process, it takes much more heat out of the air than gasoline does. Cool air is heavier, which is good. Cars produce more horsepower on cools days. Secondly, alcohol can be compressed harder and it burns at an even slower rate than gasoline."

The disadvantage of alcohol is that it takes twice as much as gasoline. At Indy, alcohol is preferred for its cooling effect and horsepower, plus the fact that it doesn't ignite as easily in a crash.

Fire has always been a major fear of racing drivers. Many have died in flames, but none so tragically as Davie MacDonald and Eddie Sachs at Indy in 1964. Sachs drove into MacDonald's crashing car because there was no visibility in the orange flames and black smoke. Sachs's car was built with

Every precaution possible is taken to prevent fire.

a fuel tank in the nose and it exploded like a bomb. After that, many people wanted gasoline banned.

Today for safety, fuel tank size is restricted to force cars to carry less fuel. The cars hold forty gallons, so pit stops are frequent. Everyone agrees that required fuel stops give Indy another exciting feature: watching crews compete for the perfect pit stop. Thirty-five gallons will flow through a four-inch hose in eleven seconds. Only five gallons of the forty can be on the right—or wall side—of the car, reducing the fire hazard should the car hit the wall. In most modern ground effects cars, the fuel tanks have been moved behind the driver. Today the fire danger that has claimed so many lives in the past is minimal.

Have you ever watched on TV as men with fuel hoses and wheels rush around a car and service it, sending it back onto the track with new tires and a full tank in seconds? Let's talk to crew man Jonesy Morris and find out what those men do.

Pit Stops

Many a race has been won or lost by the men in the pits. In the early days, the riding mechanic who looked over the driver's shoulder to warn him of approaching cars also had to pump fuel to the engine and watch for tire wear. If the car broke a part or ran out of gas, he ran to the pits to get the tools and parts to repair the car or lugged back enough fuel to get the car moving. After 1938, drivers no longer had a riding mechanic.

Modern Champ car racing depends on precision pit stops. These stops are one of the most exciting challenges at the race track. After the car squeals to a halt in the pit lane, the car is serviced and returned to the competition, often in less than twenty seconds.

There are five members on the team that come over the wall to the car. Any other help—holding out a cup of water or picking debris from a radiator—has to be done with a long pole. Most Champ car drivers don't take a drink during a race because the modern helmet covers the mouth.

The five men are the right front tire man, the jack man, the rear tire man, the vent man, and the refueling man. Their routine chores are changing tires and refueling. Let's look at each man's job, examining how he does it quickly.

Interscope pit crew change right side tires.

There are two ways that a crew can tell a driver where to stop the car. Some teams use a *stop man* to show the driver where to stop. In addition to the five men over the wall, this man stands with his body behind the wall, holding a long pole with the driver's number on the end. The other approach is for the *right front tire man* to stand at the head of the pit area where he wants the car to stop.

Cars at Indy must come to a stop before the crew jumps over the wall to work. This is because of the long hose on the pneumatic (nitrogen driven) wrenches used to remove tires. If the car runs over the hose, the driver is given a one lap penalty. The hoses have a thirty pound wrench on the end, and in the past cars have snagged them in their rush to leave, sending them sailing dangerously through the pits.

The right front tire man also puts a mark on the pit lane. Cars are not allowed to go more than one car length past their pit. If they do, then they have to leave the pit area and go around the track to try again. If they go too far, but not so far that they have to make another lap, the right front tire man looks at his mark and yells: "Push back!"

Jonesy tells why. "You aren't allowed to have a very long hose on the refueling rig. The crew must push the car back in order to reach the tank."

When the car comes to a stop in the proper place, the right front tire man kneels down and takes off the single nut that holds on the wheel. Champ cars use a "captive nut." This is either a large nut that stays attached to the wheel or a large nut that remains in the socket on the wrench. He sets the wrench down in front of him when the nut is off, puts the tire to his left, reaches to the right for the new wheel and tire and puts it on. The right front wheel is small enough for one man to handle this chore. Then he changes the direction of the pneumatic wrench to tighten the nut. This takes place in only eleven seconds!

While this is going on, the *jack man* and the *rear tire man* are working together. Rear tires are larger and more difficult to handle. Right side tires wear out much faster than those on the left because of the left turn design of the tracks. There are two common procedures to change rear tires.

Close-up of the air jacks.

    The jack man can jack up the car using an over center manual jack called a quick jack. This jack works like a lever to lift the car in one motion rather than a series of pumping motions like the jack used in a garage. When he is doing this, the rear tire man is taking off the wheel. Or the car may be equipped with *air jacks*. Air jacks are jacks that are built into the car and are activated by an air hose. One of the advantages of air jacks is when a left side tire must be changed. It is difficult to get a manual jack into place between the car and the wall. One of the disadvantages of air jacks is sometimes there is a hesitation before the car returns to the ground. The driver loses valuable fractions of a second waiting for the car to be lowered. A rear tire change can be done in fifteen seconds. When these two men are done, they prepare to push the car away, which helps the driver not to stall the engine and makes it easier on the clutch.

Old-time race crew pose with their race car and transport.

The fourth man is the *vent man*. The vent man works with the *refueling man*. An "empty" tank isn't really empty. It is filled with air. Venting the tank is necessary because the air inside the tank must be replaced with fuel. When the refueling man sees fuel appear in the plastic vent hose, he knows that the tank is full. Some teams use a timed method of putting in fuel. "This is riskier," Jonesy tells us, "because it is possible to go through the whole routine and not get any fuel in the car at all. The dry break couplings that are used on the fuel tanks to prevent spillage can be very stubborn. If the hose isn't jammed in hard enough, it may be that no fuel is going in. Also the fuel flows much faster early in the race when the overhead rig is full."

In Champ car races, the cars are allotted a certain amount of fuel, enough for 1.8 miles per gallon. They must be careful not to use more than that by producing too much horsepower by turning up the engine boost to go faster or by wasting fuel. After each stop, the vent man will hold his hose up high, allowing the precious fuel to drain back into the rig tank for the next stop.

Jonesy tells us: "Any problem other than changing wheels and putting in fuel usually ends your chances of winning the race. Sometimes a quick adjustment to the front wing is possible, but rear wing changes take too long. It is crucial for the crew not to make a mistake or give the driver a miscue. At Phoenix in 1980, Rick Mears left the pits before his rear tire man had tightened the nut, losing a wheel before he got to the track."

Drivers can talk to their crew chief on two-way radios that fit into the driver's helmet. Teams still use pit boards held beside the track because the car's ignition and engine can overpower the radio. The crew can spot handling problems. "You have to watch the car," Jonesy says, "because the radios often malfunction and only work well in the pit straight area." In the 1981 Indy 500, Bobby Unser's radio went out on the start and he received all of his pit signals from the board man.

As you can see, racing is a team sport. Every job from fine tuning an engine to changing a tire is one step on the road to victory.

Near the end of the 1982 Indy 500, a photographer was rushed to the finish line for a possible photo finish. The closest race in Indy history had happened forty years ago when only two seconds separated the first and second place cars. Gordon Johncock, 1973 Indy winner and now a grandfather, and 1979 winner Rick Mears in the incredible Penske PC-10, a car that had set a record lap in the race averaging over 200 mph, were in a dead heat on the next to last lap. Johncock leapt ahead in the first turn, taking his Wildcat through a series of brilliant maneuvers. He moved up and down on the slippery track, watching his mirrors to keep Mears behind. When he saw the checkered flag, Johncock crossed the finish line .16 of a second ahead of Mears, the closest finish in Indy history.

In 500 miles the cars travel 2,640,000 feet and Johncock had won by only 20 feet!

Times have changed at Indy and on the Championship Trail for Champ cars. Today's race cars go more than twice the speed of their ancestors. "Gasoline Alley" could be called "Alcohol Alley." The "Brickyard" has been covered with asphalt. But one thing has stayed the same—there is no greater spectacle in sports than Champ cars racing the Indy 500.

Howdy Holmes (30) and Bobby Rahal (19) in March-Cosworths.

Glossary

AAA: American Automobile Association, sanctioned Indy racing until 1955 when USAC (United States Auto Club) was formed

aerodynamics: the branch of dynamics that deals with the force of air on a moving object, such as a race car

alcohol: fuel used in Champ cars, also called methanol

banking: degree of inclination or angle of the road in a turn

bondo: body putty used to fill dents in street cars before repainting; also used to form the shape of a newly designed race car body (see plug)

boost: the pressure of the air/fuel mixture entering a supercharged engine in excess of atmospheric pressure

bubble: the car/driver who has made the field of thirty-three cars with the slowest qualifying speed is said to be on the bubble. He will be the first to be bumped if his speed is bettered, breaking his bubble. (see bump)

buck: the wooden skeleton used as the frame for a plug (see plug, station)

bump: when a non-qualified driver qualifies fast enough to make an already full starting lineup, he is said to "bump" the car/driver he replaces from the grid.

CART: Championship Auto Racing Teams; a group of car owners who broke away from USAC, feeling USAC did not act in their best interest; use the SCCA (Sports Car Club of America) to sanction their races

Champ car: also called Indy, Championship car; a high powered, single seat, open cockpit and open-wheel car used in North American competition, primarily oval tracks such as Indianapolis and Pocono, some road racing

chassis: the frame upon which is mounted the body of a car, the understructure of a car. This is a confusing term meaning everything from a frame to a full car. In racing, if you purchase a chassis (or rolling chassis), you can expect a monocoque, suspension, wheels, body, and drive train but no engine.

chute: straight part of the race track

clutch: the controllable link used to engage or disengage the engine from the rest of the drive train

cockpit: the space in the race car where the driver is seated with access to the manual controls—steering wheel, gear shifter, brake, throttle, etc.

cornering: the act of driving through a turn

Cosworth DFX V-8: turbocharged version of the Formula One engine (Cosworth DFV), the most common engine in today's Champ cars

crew: the members of a team, only five of whom are allowed to work on the car during a pit stop

crew chief: the mechanic in charge of car preparation who directs the individual members of the team, the foreman on a racing team

downforce, download: the desirable force produced by air passing over and under a moving race car that presses the car to the ground (for opposite, see lift)

driver restraint system: a system of six belts that hook into a common buckle, two around the waist, two over the shoulders, and one or two through the crotch. This harness must be used whenever the vehicle is on the track.

dry-break: a coupling at the entrance to the fuel tank that is designed to prevent spillage during refueling

engine displacement: the size of an engine, measured in cubic inches (ci., cu. ins.), cubic centimeters (cc.), cubic inch displacement (CID, c.i.d.), or liters, not including combustion chamber size

fabricator: a highly skilled worker who builds new structures or improves existing structures

fiber glass/fiberglass: fiber glass is glass in a bendable fiber form. When it is combined with resin and a catalyst (a substance used to cause a chemical reaction), it becomes fiberglass, a hard, lightweight substance used for race car bodies.

fiberglass mold: a mold used to form fiberglass into a desired shape

front row: At Indy, the first, second, and third qualifiers make up the front row of the grid. Each row consists of three cars. On the road courses and shorter tracks, each row has two cars.

fuel cell: the fire-safety container to hold fuel in a race car that consists of a metal or plastic structure with a rubber bladder filled with sponge-like material

Grand Prix, Formula One car: a high powered, advanced design, single seat, open cockpit, open-wheel race car used in international road racing competition, such as Monaco and Long Beach

g-force, gravity force: one g, or one gravity, is the weight of each object resting on the earth's surface. If an object is subjected to acceleration, the resulting force acting on the object is measured in g's. In a race car the driver feels this force acting on his body as he corners, accelerates, or brakes.

grid: the starting positions of cars in a race as determined by qualifying

groove: the fastest route around an oval. Road racers use a different word—line. There is one difference in the two terms: track conditions can cause the groove to change, while line seldom varies.

ground effects: an aerodynamic approach in modern race cars that achieves downforce from the way air passes between a specially curved bottomside on the car and the ground (or road) producing a low pressure area under the car

handling: the car's reaction to the manual controls, i.e., braking, accelerating, steering

helmet: protective head and face covering consisting of a hard shell with foam liner and chin strap

horsepower: standard unit of power used to measure engine output, equal to 746 watts and 550 foot-pounds of work per second

independent suspension: a suspension system that isolates each wheel

infield: the inner area of an oval track often used by the competitors for pits and paddock

lap: a complete circuit of a race course

lift: in racing, an undesirable force that reduces a car's ability to adhere to the ground; lift is what an airplane has on take off (for opposite, see downforce)

loose: tendency of a car to steer into a turn more than intended with the rear end losing adhesion and swinging to the outside, also called oversteer (for opposite see push)

Magnaflux: trademark, method of checking a ferrous (containing iron) metal for defects or cracks. Racing components are magnafluxed frequently to head off a failure under stress.

Mini-Indy: a professional series for Super Vee begun in 1977, run in conjunction with Champ car races

monocoque: a construction technique used extensively in the aircraft industry and widely adopted by race car designers (called fuselage on an airplane, tub or chassis on a race car); a monocoque structure is made very rigid and strong without using a heavy framework but by using its light sheet metal skin (stressed skin) to form a strong, light unit

Nomex: trademark, a fire resistant fabric used in driver's clothing (also refueling crews) for socks, shoes, underwear, head socks, helmet liners, gloves, and coveralls

Offy, Offenhauser: an almost extinct brand of American racing engines that for years was the best

open-wheel: without fenders

oval: an oval-shaped race track

overhead rig: a large fuel reservoir set up in the pits on a tall platform using a long hose (gravity feed) to refuel race cars. Overhead rigs are used for long races where large quantities of fuel will be used.

pace car: a car used to lead the competitors in a race through a pace or warm-up lap; does not participate in the race, pulling off the track before the green flag waves. Also can be used for a restart after a caution period.

pace lap: a lap taken by the competitors before the start of a race to warm up the cars and to prepare for a moving start. This is sometimes mistakenly called a parade lap. A parade lap is a much slower lap preceding the pace lap to allow the spectators to see the cars.

pits: the pit area is beside the race track, usually on a straight, and is used for refueling and servicing the cars

pit board: a hand-held signal board used by a crew member to give a driver information in abbreviated form as he passes. Examples: E-Z means take it easy, 2 in or 2⟶ means come in in two laps.

plug: a metal, wood, and full-scale reproduction of a race car, used as the foundation for a fiberglass mold

pneumatic wrench: a heavy-duty nitrogen driven wrench used on race car wheel nuts

pole position: the number one qualifier, the inside position

push: tendency of a car to steer less sharply than intended, with the front end tending to go straight, also called understeer (for opposite, see loose)

qualifying: an on-track session where a driver demonstrates his speed in relation to other car/driver combinations, determining his starting position and/or whether he can reach the speed required to run the race

racing slick: a wide, treadless tire used for racing only

radiator: a nest of tubes with a large surface area exposed to moving air to cool its circulating fluid contents: water or oil (also called oil cooler) that were heated by friction inside the engine and transmission

road racing: a form of racing that takes place on a closed circuit track designed to resemble a country road with a variety of turns and hills

roadster: a front engine Indy car of the mid-fifties to early sixties which passed the driveshaft beside the driver instead of beneath him to lower the car

roll bar: a metal hoop in a race car to protect the driver in a roll over.

rolling, flying start: start of a race where the cars are moving in formation at speed when the green flag waves

rookie: a driver in his first season of racing. An experienced driver is called a veteran. A veteran can become a rookie again if he tries a different form of racing. For example, Richard Petty would be called a rookie if he tried to race at Indy.

sidepod: a structure on each side of a car that has a ground effects panel on the bottomside and often carries radiators, oil coolers, etc., within

spin: to go out of control and revolve. A driver can "spin out" and stay on course, or "spin off" the track.

stagger: when a tire on one side of a car is larger than a tire on the other side, it has stagger. Stagger is the difference in the circumference of the two tires.

station: a cross member in a wooden buck (see buck)

stick, bite: in racing terms, stick means adhesion in general, Example: the tires are sticking well. Bite means traction coming off a turn. Example: The rear tires were getting more bite or The car was sticking well in the rear.

stock car: an unmodified car, just as it came off the assembly line. That is the dictionary definition, but a stock car used in NASCAR racing by drivers like Richard Petty is a highly modified car. So, if you mean "unmodified" say *the car is stock*; if you mean what Petty drives, say *stock car*.

Super Vee: a small, approximately 950 lbs., open-wheel, single seat, rear engine racer using the VW Rabbit engine and many VW parts

suspension: the system of springs, shocks, and linkages that suspend the main structure of a car from the wheels

tri-oval: a variation of the pure oval track with a curve in the start-finish straight making the track triangular

turbocharger screw: the device used in adjusting the amount of boost or pressure that the turbocharger forces into the engine (see boost)

USAC: United States Auto Club, group that sanctions Indy

vent hose: a hose attached to one of the fuel tank dry-break couplings during refueling to allow the air in the cell to escape without fuel spillage

Victory Circle: an area on or beside the track where the winner goes after the race to receive his award, kiss the queen, and pose for photos

visor: a clear or tinted plastic eye protection; thin visors are often worn in layers and can be torn off as they become dirty (called tearoffs)

wheel hammer: a heavy hammer used to secure and loosen wheel nuts

wing: an aerodynamic structure used on the rear and sometimes on the front (called wing or canard) of a racing car to produce downforce for better traction

Index

accidents, 21, 33, 34
aerodynamics, 14
air jacks, 39
"Alcohol Alley," 42
alcohol fuel, 34
Andretti, Mario, 29
Ascari, Alberto, 32
bladders, fuel containers, 30
board man, 41
bodies, fiberglass, 16
bondo, 16
Brabham, Jack, 14
Brawner, Clint, 14, 29
"Brickyard," 21, 42
Carlson, Willie, 34
Champ car tracks, 21-23
Chapman, Colin, 14, 16
Chevrolet brothers, Gaston and Louis, 29

Clark, Jimmy, 15
Climax engine, 14
closed circuit tracks, 21
concentration, 26, 27
crew, racing, 36-41
curved-bottom cars, 18, 19
Darlington race track, 23
Daytona race track, 23
De Palma, Ralph, 10
downforce, 18
Drake, Dale, 12
driving the Indy 500, 24-42
Eagle race car, 18
endurance, 25
engines, Champ cars, 3, 12, 14, 15
Ferrari race car, 32
fiberglass bodies, 16
fires, 34

Firestone, Dennis, 5, 6-8, 20, 24, 27, 33
Firestone Tire Company, 15
first Indy 500 race, 1911, 9, 10, 21, 30
Fisher, Carl, 9, 21
flat-bottom cars, 18, 20
foreign drivers, 10
Formula One race cars, 14, 22
Foyt, A. J., 5, 29
front engines, 12, 15
fuel, 34, 35, 41
fuel containers, 30, 35
fuel stops, 35
fuel tanks 30, 35
"Funny Car," 14, 15
garages, 3, 34
"Gasoline Alley," 3, 34, 42
gasoline fuel, 34, 35

g-forces (gravity forces), 20, 23
Goux (French driver), 10
Grand Prix racing, 12, 22
ground effects, 12, 18-20, 35
Hall of Fame, 7
Harroun, Ray, 30
helmets, 32, 41
hose, pneumatic wrench, 37
hose, refueling, 38
Indianapolis, Indiana, 3, 21
Indianapolis 500, 3-15, 20, 21-23, 24-42
Indianapolis Raceway Park, 6
Indianapolis Speedway, 5, 6
jack man, 36, 38, 39
jacks, air, 39
jacks, quick, 39
Johncock, Gordon, 42
Jones, Parnelli, 29
kerosene fuel, 34
Lotus-Ford race cars, 14, 15, 16
"low profile" tires, 15
MacDonald, Davie, 34
magnaflux, 30
Maxwell race car, 34
McCoy, Wiley, 34
Mears, Rick, 41, 42
mechanics, riding, 21, 30, 36
Memorial Day, 3
mental fatigue, 26
Mercedes, 10
methonol fuel, 34
Meyer, Louis, 12
Michigan race track, 22
Mini-Indy race, 6

mirror, rear view, 30
monocoque construction, 12, 16
Monroe race car, 29
Morris, Jonesy, 28, 35, 38, 40, 41
Mulford, Ralph, 10
Museum, Speedway, 21
Offy engine, 12
open road tracks, 21
oval tracks, 22, 23
parade lap, 8
PC7 Champ car, 18
Penske, Roger, 18
Penske PC-10 race car, 42
Phoenix race track, 41
photo finish, 1982 Indy 500 race, 42
pit boards, 41
pit stops, 28, 29, 35, 36-41
plug (foundation for fiberglass mold), 16
Pocno race track, 22, 23
purse, Indy 500, 3, 9, 10
qualifying runs, 5
quick jacks, 39
racing crew, 36-41
racing team, 36-41
radios, two-way, 41
rear engines, 12, 14, 15
rear tire man, 36, 38
rear view mirror, 30
refueling, 36, 40, 41
refueling man, 36, 40
riding mechanics, 21, 30, 36
right front tire man, 36-38
Riverside race track, 22

road courses, 22
rookie tests, 5, 33
Rutherford, Johnny, 5
Sachs, Eddie, 5, 29, 34
safety, 30-32, 34, 35
seat belt systems, 30
Shaw, Wilbur, 31, 32, 34
sidepods, 19
Sneva, Tom, 5, 20, 23, 24, 25-27
Speedway, 5, 6
Speedway Museum, 21
spoked wheels, 31, 32
stop man, 37
strategy, 27
suits, flame-resistant, 32
Super Vee race cars, 5, 6, 24
Talledega race track, 23
team, racing, 36-41
temperatures, inside race cars, 27
tires, changing, 36-39
tires, "low profile," 15
tracks, Champ car, 21-23
tri-oval tracks, 22
Unser, Al, 5
Unser, Bobby, 5, 18, 41
vent man, 36, 40, 41
Victory Circle, 29
Vukovich, Bill, 24
wheels, changing, 38, 39
wheels, wire or spoked, 31, 32
Wildcat race car, 42
wing, race car, 18, 19, 41
wire wheels, 31, 32
wrenches, pneumatic, 37, 38

About the Author
Sylvia Wilkinson was born in Durham, North Carolina and studied at the University of North Carolina, Hollins College, and Stanford University. She has taught at UNC, William and Mary, Sweet Briar College, and held numerous writer-in-residence posts. Her awards include a Eugene Saxton Memorial Trust Grant, A Wallace Stegner Creative Writing Fellowship, a *Mademoiselle* Merit Award for Literature, two Sir Walter Raleigh Awards for Literature, a National Endowment for the Arts Grant, and a Guggenheim Fellowship. In addition to four novels, she has written a nonfiction work on auto racing: *The Stainless Steel Carrot;* an adventure series on auto racing; an education handbook; and articles for *Sports Illustrated, Mademoiselle, Ingenue, True, The American Scholar, The Writer,* and others. Her four novels: *Moss on the North Side, A Killing Frost, Cale,* and *Shadow of the Mountain* are available in Pocket editions. A fifth novel, *Bone of My Bones,* was recently published by G.P. Putnam's.

Sylvia Wilkinson is head timer and scorer for Paul Newman's Can-Am racing team. She also times the Daytona 24-hour and Le Mans.